Insects
Fireflies

Launch!
An Imprint of Abdo Zoom
abdobooks.com

Leo Statts

abdobooks.com

Published by Abdo Zoom, a division of ABDO, PO Box 398166, Minneapolis, Minnesota 55439.
Copyright © 2019 by Abdo Consulting Group, Inc. International copyrights reserved in all countries.
No part of this book may be reproduced in any form without written permission from the publisher.
Launch!™ is a trademark and logo of Abdo Zoom.

Printed in the United States of America, North Mankato, Minnesota.

092018
012019

THIS BOOK CONTAINS
RECYCLED MATERIALS

Photo Credits: AnimalsAnimals, iStock, Shutterstock

Production Contributors: Kenny Abdo, Jennie Forsberg, Grace Hansen, John Hansen

Design Contributors: Dorothy Toth, Neil Klinepier

Library of Congress Control Number: 2018945594

Publisher's Cataloging-in-Publication Data

Names: Statts, Leo, author.

Title: Fireflies / by Leo Statts.

Description: Minneapolis, Minnesota : Abdo Zoom, 2019 | Series: Insects |
    Includes online resources and index.

Identifiers: ISBN 9781532125089 (lib. bdg.) | ISBN 9781641856539 (pbk) |
    ISBN 9781532126109 (ebook) | ISBN 9781532126611 (Read-to-me ebook)

Subjects: LCSH: Fireflies--Juvenile literature. | Lightning bugs--Juvenile
    literature. | Insects--Anatomy--Juvenile literature. | Insects--Juvenile literature.

Classification: DDC 595.7644--dc23

Table of Contents

Fireflies

Fireflies are beetles. There are more than 2,000 known species of fireflies.

Fireflies have a special body part that glows. Some fireflies can glow in different colors.

Body

Fireflies have three main body parts. They have a head, **thorax**, and **abdomen**.

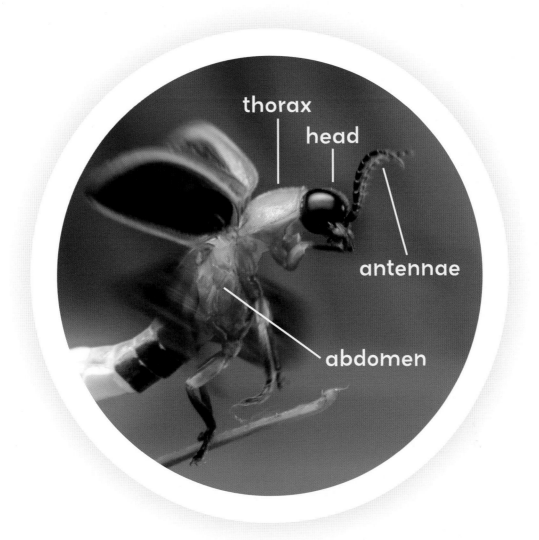

thorax

head

antennae

abdomen

Fireflies use their antennae to smell and feel things.

Habitat

They like **humid** and warm weather. It helps fireflies glow brighter and survive.

Most fireflies fly at night. They rest in the grass during the day.

Food

Adult fireflies only eat **nectar** and pollen from plants.

Fireflies are carnivores when they are larvae.

A **larva** eats worms and insects. It also eats snails.

The **larva** sprays poison into its **prey**. This turns its prey into juice that it can drink.

Life Cycle

Female fireflies lay many eggs. Firefly **larvae** hatch from those eggs.

A firefly is a **larva** for one to two years.

Then it changes into a **pupa**.
The pupa's skin splits open
and an adult firefly crawls out.

Average Length

A firefly is about the same size as a penny.

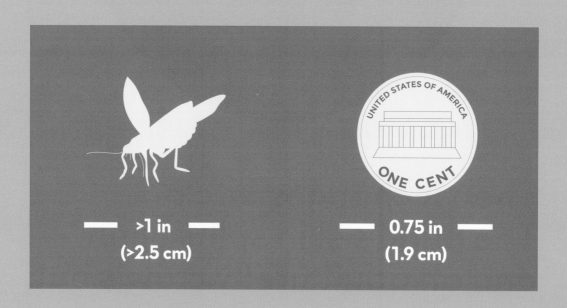

>1 in
(>2.5 cm)

0.75 in
(1.9 cm)

Fun Fact

Fireflies breathe through tiny holes in their abdomens.

Glossary

abdomen – the back part of an insect's body.

antennae – the two long, thin "feelers" on an insect's head.

carnivore – an animal that eats flesh.

larva – an animal in a very young form.

nectar – a sweet liquid, or sugar water, that flowering plants make.

prey – an animal hunted or killed by a predator for food.

pupa – an insect that is changing from a larva into an adult.

thorax – the middle part of an insect's body.

Online Resources

For more information on fireflies, please visit **abdobooklinks.com**

Learn even more with the Abdo Zoom Animals database. Visit **abdozoom.com** today!

Index